Shapes Everywhere

Shapes in Nature

Oona Gaarder-Juntti

Consulting Editor, Diane Craig, M.A./Reading Specialist

A Division of ABDO

ABDO
Publishing Company

visit us at www.abdopublishing.com

Published by ABDO Publishing Company, a division of ABDO, P.O. Box 398166, Minneapolis, Minnesota 55439.

Printed in the United States of America, North Mankato, Minnesota
062013
012014

 PRINTED ON RECYCLED PAPER

Editor: Liz Salzmann
Content Developer: Nancy Tuminelly
Cover and Interior Design and Production: Oona Gaarder-Juntti, Mighty Media, Inc.
Photo Credits: Ablestock.com, Brand X Pictures, Comstock, Creatas Images, Hemera Technologies, Jupiterimages, PhotoObjects.net, Shutterstock, Stockbyte, Thinkstock

Library of Congress Cataloging-in-Publication Data
Gaarder-Juntti, Oona, 1979-
  Shapes in nature / Oona Gaarder-Juntti.
      p. cm. -- (Shapes everywhere)
  ISBN 978-1-61783-414-1
  1. Shapes--Juvenile literature. 2. Geometry in nature--Juvenile literature. I. Title.
  QA445.5.G337 2013
  516'.15--dc23
                                    2011051114

Super SandCastle™ books are created by a team of professional educators, reading specialists, and content developers around five essential components—phonemic awareness, phonics, vocabulary, text comprehension, and fluency—to assist young readers as they develop reading skills and strategies and increase their general knowledge. All books are written, reviewed, and leveled for guided reading, early reading intervention, and Accelerated Reader® programs for use in shared, guided, and independent reading and writing activities to support a balanced approach to literacy instruction.

Table of Contents

Shapes Are Everywhere 4

2-D or 3-D? 5

Star 6

Oval 8

Circle 10

Sphere 12

Cone 14

Triangle 16

Pyramid.................................... 18

Hexagon 20

Shapes! 22

How Many? 23

Glossary 24

Shapes Are Everywhere

Shapes are everywhere in nature! Here are some shapes you might see. Let's learn more about shapes.

2-D or 3-D?

2-Dimensional Shapes

Some shapes are two-dimensional,
or 2-D. A 2-D shape is flat.
You can draw it on a piece of paper.

**circle
2-D shape**

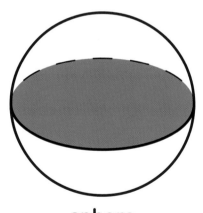

**sphere
3-D shape**

3-Dimensional Shapes

Some shapes are three-dimensional,
or 3-D. A 3-D shape takes up space.
You can hold a 3-D shape in your hands.

STAR

A starfish is in the shape of a star. Britney sees a lot of starfish when the tide is low. She puts them back into the water.

OVAL

Peacocks have ovals on their tail feathers. They look like eyes. Cody sees peacocks at the zoo.

CIRCLE

The center of a sunflower is a circle. Morgan likes taking pictures of sunflowers. The bright yellow color makes her happy.

SPHERE

The **insect** eggs are spheres.
Lucy learns about different
insects at the nature center.
She watches insect eggs **hatch**.

CONE

The rhinoceros has a **horn** shaped like a cone. Colin and his family are on an African **safari**. He can't believe how huge rhinoceroses are!

TRIANGLE

The bird's **beaks** are triangles. There is a nest in a tree in Sean's backyard. He watches the baby birds. They cry out for food.

PYRAMID

Some of the **crystals** form pyramids. Kylie collects rocks and crystals. She wants to be a **geologist** when she grows up.

HEXAGON

The holes in a **honeycomb** are hexagons. Isaac's uncle is a beekeeper. He sells the honey the bees make.

Shapes!

Here are the shapes in this book, plus a few more.
Look for them in nature!

diamond

rectangle

pentagon

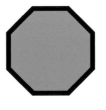

hexagon

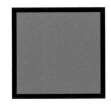

octagon

square

star

heart

oval

triangle

circle

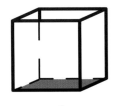

cube

sphere

cylinder

cone

pyramid

How Many?

How many shapes can you find in this picture?

Glossary

beak – the hard, projecting jaws of a bird.

crystal – a type of mineral or rock that light can shine through.

geologist – someone whose job is to study the earth and how it changes over time.

hatch – to break out of an egg.

honeycomb – a structure that bees make out of wax.

horn – a hard, bony growth on the head of an animal.

insect – a small creature with two or four wings, six legs, and a body with three sections.

safari – a trip taken to see large wild animals, especially in Africa.